Thank You, Baobab Tree!

Written by Mi-hwa Joo
Illustrated by Yun-heu Park
Edited by Joy Cowley

big & SMALL

DATE DUE 4/16

Smash!

I scored a goal!
"Yes!" I yelled. "We've won!"

"Well done, Slupu!"
shouted my friends.

I gave them a thumbs up.

2

We were hot after the game,
so we jumped into the sea.
We soon cooled down.
I said to my friend Dopin,
"After lunch, let's go and play."

Once we'd eaten, Dopin and I
went to the playground.
On the way, we found
a couple of chameleons.
My chameleon was small
but it had nice black dots
on its bright green body.
I wanted to ask my sister
whose chameleon was best.

My sister and her friends
sat under a baobab tree.
They were making bags
from the bark they had stripped
off the old baobab tree.
My sister made good bags.

The bags are made from string
pulled from baobab tree bark.

8

Dopin and I decided to race our chameleons.
The chameleons moved very slowly.
At first, my chameleon was slower than Dopin's,
but then his chameleon stopped.
My chameleon won the race.
Dopin wasn't very pleased.

When I went into my baobab tree hole,
Dopin tried to follow me. I said to him,
"This is my tree. Go and find your own!"

"No, this is my tree," he shouted.
My sister called, "Be nice to each other!"

When he heard that, Dopin walked inside.

People in Madagascar often use hollows in baobab trees to store things – or even as a house.

I didn't want to speak to Dopin
so I played a tune on my guitar.
Dopin started singing loudly,
his voice echoing in the tree hole.
The girls outside began singing too,
which made me laugh. This was fun.

14

"I'm hungry," I said to my sister.

She gave me a fruit that had fallen
from my baobab tree. "Take this, Slupu."

I shared the white inside of the fruit
with Dopin, and I said to him,
"Say thanks to my baobab tree."

He didn't answer. He just got up
and ran away without a word.

17

I wanted to chase him,
but my sister stopped me.
Dopin hid so I couldn't see him.
That didn't matter because
I could hear his hiccups.
He always got hiccups
when he was nervous.

When I found Dopin, he was angry.
He shouted, "It isn't just your tree!
That baobab belongs to everyone!"
He walked away, huffing and puffing.

No one was at home when I got back.
I sat alone, thinking of Grandma
who passed away last year.
She once told me I was very sick
when I was a little boy,
and she had fed me medicine
made from baobab leaves.
Grandma had called the baobab tree
a "Slupu tree" ever since.

 African people use baobab leaves as medicine.

I went outside and did a handstand
beside my Slupu baobab tree.
Dopin was right. It belonged to everyone.
Maybe Grandma called it a Slupu tree
because she wanted me to help people
just the way this tree helped people.
I had to tell Dopin what I thought.
But first I said, "Thank you, baobab tree!"

About Madagascar
The Land of Baobab Trees

The white panel in the flag of Madagascar represents freedom, the red stands for patriotism and the green for progression. This flag was created after the country gained independence from France in 1959.

Home of Baobab Trees

There are eight species of baobab trees in the world and all eight can be found in Madagascar. A baobab tree can grow so big that ten adults can't stretch their arms around the trunk. The upper branches spread out, making them look like roots growing in the sky. Baobabs can live for between 1,000 and 5,000 years, and Madagascans rely on baobab trees for many things. That is why Madagascans call them the "trees of life."

An avenue of baobab trees in Morondava, a city in west Madagascar.

Fruit of the baobab tree

The Giving Tree

These trees provide a lot for the people of Madagascar. Their fruits are eaten, both fresh and roasted, and they are made into juice. The seeds are crushed to extract oil and make soap. Their leaves and bark are used as medicine. Tree bark fibres are knotted to make bags, ropes, fishing nets and clothing. A hollow baobab tree trunk provides a shelter.

The Color of Chameleons

A chameleon can change its body color depending on how it feels. It also catches insects with its long tongue, and although it can't hear well, its vision is highly developed. It searches for prey with its separately moving eyes. About half of all chameleon species live in Madagascar, their sizes varying from as small as a human finger to as big as an arm.

A chameleon in Madagascar

The Sea, a Source of Life

Madagascar is an island with seas surrounding it. Many people live by the sea, and people on the western coast near the Mozambique Channel rely on fishing. Children collect shells from the beaches and sell them. The shells go to places like Europe and make attractive ornaments and accessories.

Traditional Madagascan fishing boat in the Mozambique Channel.

People Living with Nature

Madagascar is the fourth largest island in the world. The climate varies greatly according to the region. There are tropical, temperate, arid and wet areas, and many unique animals and plants are found in Madagascar. But, with the increasing number of tourists, some of the wildlife is in danger of becoming extinct. The people of Madagascar are trying to protect their natural environment by establishing national parks and prohibited areas.

Tsingy de Bemaraha Strict Nature Reserve

Rice, a Staple Food

For most Africans, corn is their main food, but people in Madagascar eat rice. Because there are few plains for growing rice, people cut terraces in the hills to make paddies for rice farming.

Rice growing on terraced land in Madagascar.

Lemurs in Madagascar

Madagascar is well-known for lemurs, animals which aren't found anywhere else. They have a long snout and mouth, and a bushy tail. They eat leaves, fruit and insects. It lives in female-led groups.

A ring-tailed lemur in Madagascar

Angonoka Tortoise

Angonoka tortoises, unique to Madagascar, are considered by many to be the most beautiful of all tortoises. They have a highly domed shell with prominent growth rings. The shell is dark brown with bright yellow and orange lines. These tortoises are critically endangered so the species is greatly protected.

Angonoka tortoises

Isalo National Park

Isalo National Park stretches across the island from north to south. Among the grasslands and tropical forests, the rocks and cliffs are carved into strange shapes from being buffeted by centuries of wind and water. The park is home to many unique plants and animals, like the ring-tailed lemur.

Isalo National Park, Madagascar

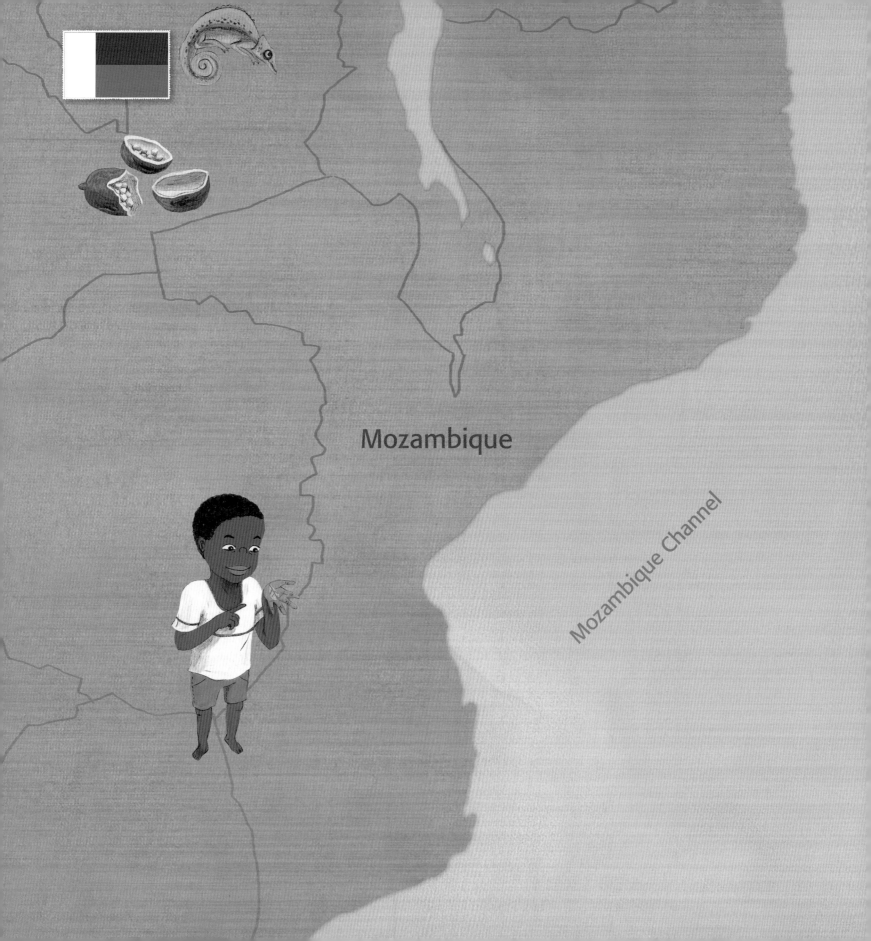

Mozambique

Mozambique Channel

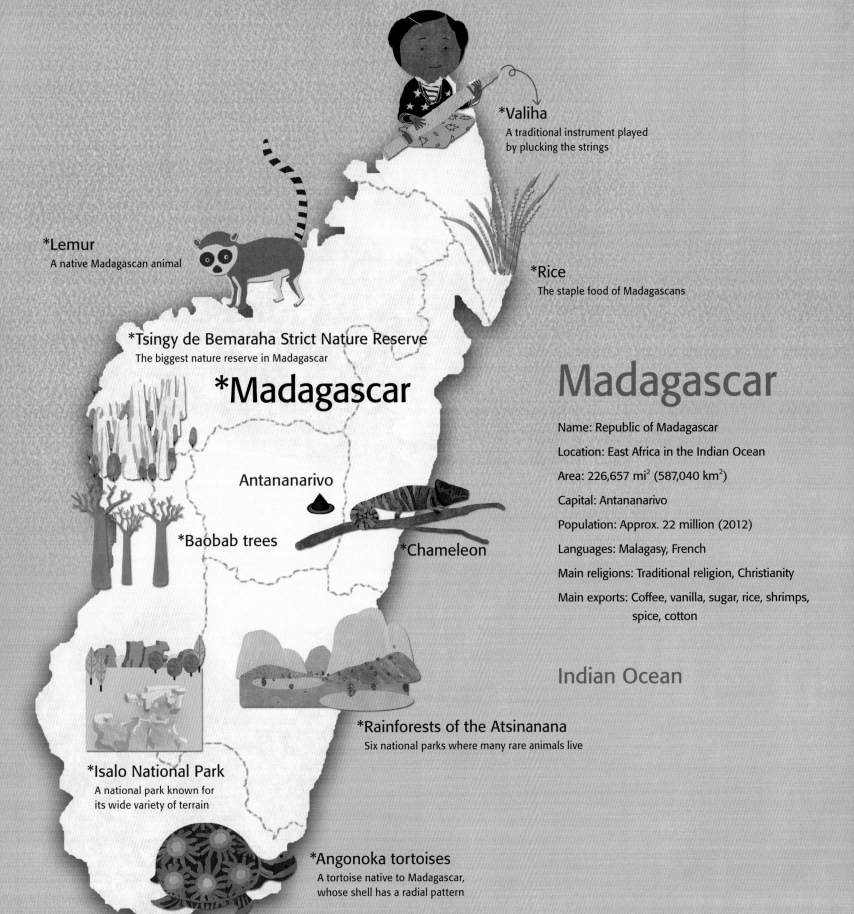

*Valiha
A traditional instrument played
by plucking the strings

*Lemur
A native Madagascan animal

*Rice
The staple food of Madagascans

*Tsingy de Bemaraha Strict Nature Reserve
The biggest nature reserve in Madagascar

*Madagascar

Antananarivo

*Baobab trees

*Chameleon

*Isalo National Park
A national park known for
its wide variety of terrain

*Rainforests of the Atsinanana
Six national parks where many rare animals live

*Angonoka tortoises
A tortoise native to Madagascar,
whose shell has a radial pattern

Madagascar

Name: Republic of Madagascar

Location: East Africa in the Indian Ocean

Area: 226,657 mi² (587,040 km²)

Capital: Antananarivo

Population: Approx. 22 million (2012)

Languages: Malagasy, French

Main religions: Traditional religion, Christianity

Main exports: Coffee, vanilla, sugar, rice, shrimps,
spice, cotton

Indian Ocean

Original Korean text by Mi-hwa Joo
Illustrations by Yun-heu Park
Korean edition © Aram Publishing

This English edition published by big & SMALL in 2016
by arrangement with Aram Publishing
English text edited by Joy Cowley
English edition © big & SMALL 2016

Distributed in the United States and Canada by
Lerner Publishing Group, Inc.
241 First Avenue North
Minneapolis, MN 55401 U.S.A.
www.lernerbooks.com

Images by page no. - left to right, top to bottom
Page 26: © Bernard Gagnon (CC-BY-SA-3.0); © Ton Rulkens (CC-BY-SA-2.0);
Page 27: © JialiangGao (peace-on-earth.org) (CC-BY-SA-3.0); © World Resource
Institute (CC-BY-SA-2.0); Page 28: © Alex Dunkel (Maky) (CC-BY-SA-3.0); ©
Hardscarf (CC-BY-SA-3.0); Page 29: © Alex Dunkel (Maky) (CC-BY-SA-3.0); ©
By Olivier Lejade (CC-BY-SA-2.0); © Bernard Gagnon_CC-BY-SA-3.0

ISBN: 978-1-925247-55-8

Printed in Korea